THE THEATRE ROYAL

By the same author:
The Art of the Theatre Workshop (Oberon Books, 2006)

THE THEATRE ROYAL

A History of the Building

BY

MURRAY MELVIN

Dear Ken
Lest we forget!!
love
Murray
December 2009

STRATFORD EAST PUBLICATIONS
LONDON

First published in 2009 by Stratford East Publications
Theatre Royal, Gerry Raffles Square, Stratford, London E15 1BN
Tel 020 7607 3637   Fax 020 7607 3629
e-mail: theatreroyal@stratfordeast.com
www.stratfordeast.com

A catalogue record for this book is available from the
British Library.

Front Cover Photograph:
The Auditorium, Theatre Royal Stratford – Peter Durrant

ISBN: 978-0-9564565-0-2

Printed in Great Britain by CPI Antony Rowe, Chippenham.

In Loving Memory of my parents
Maisie and Victor,
who so enjoyed all their evenings at the Royal.

ACKNOWLEDGEMENTS

I am indebted to Anne Tapper for allowing me to use extracts from Oscar Tapper's *The Other Stratford*.

The Newham Archive and Local Studies Library for permission to reproduce sections of *The Other Stratford*, published by West Ham Public Libraries Committee in 1962.

Pat O'Connor, *The Stratford Express* for permission to use extracts from the paper printed in *The Other Stratford*.

Axel Burrough of Architects Levitt Bernstein Associates Ltd for his advice.

James Hogan, Kate Longworth and Stephen Watson of Oberon Press for their generosity and kindness to me and as always their expertise.

From the Theatre Royal: Mary Ling; Karen Fisher; Carol Murphy; Mark Pritchard; Ivor Dykes.

Harry H. Greene for his sketch of the Theatre frontage.

And to all the past and present members who have passed through the Theatre and have made this history possible.

Murray Melvin
Theatre Archivist
Theatre Royal
August 2009

There is a chronological list of the plays presented at the Theatre Royal covering the period of this history on the Theatre Royal website – www.stratfordeast.com

Thank you to

 OBERON BOOKS

for typesetting, design and production

With thanks to our funding partners:

FOREWORD

I am very grateful to our distinguished Archivist Murray Melvin for agreeing to my request for a history of Theatre Royal.

So many of our patrons, those of long standing and those who enter the building for the first time, ask about its origins and its decoration.

Murray Melvin
(Photo: Richard Jopson)

Murray was a member of Joan Littlewood's famous Theatre Workshop Company in the 50s and 60s and for the past twenty years has been our Voluntary Archivist. He has collected an enormous amount of material and now has records of productions dating back to the Theatre's Grand Opening in 1884 to the present day.

I do hope you will enjoy reading this history of our famous building and that it will add to the pleasures of your visit, and that we may welcome you again in the future.

Kerry Michael
Artistic Director
Theatre Royal, 2009

Kerry Michael (Photo: Jake Green)

THE THEATRE ROYAL
STRATFORD-ATTE-BOW

*'Ours is Chaucer's Stratford, which is
rather older than Shakespeare's'*
JOAN LITTLEWOOD

THEATRE ROYAL, ANGEL LANE, STRATFORD

The actor-manager William Silver, professionally known as Charles Dillon,[1] was the son of an actress, and was connected by his sister Emily's marriage to Frederick Fredericks, an actor. Fredericks was named after his father, another actor-manager Frederick O'Leary Fredericks. In the early 1880s Dillon joined the Fredericks family in their portable theatre company or 'Fit-Up'. They appeared at fetes and fairs in East London and Essex, at the Wanstead Flats, for example, and also had a more permanent site at Oxford Road, Stratford, quite close to Salway Road.

On 5th July 1884 Charles Dillon made an application before the Stratford Magistrates for a licence to open a permanent theatre. He believed that Stratford was large enough to support such a venture, and was supported in this belief by the local newspaper the *Stratford Express*, which commented that:

> There is no provincial town of the size of Stratford without its theatre and it is rather strange that theatrical enterprise has not before now paid a little attention to it.

Dillon's planning application for the proposed theatre met with violent opposition from certain sections of the community. The Reverend R.P. Pelly, the then vicar of St John's on Stratford Broadway, rallied the opposition

---

[1] See the family tree reproduced in Anne Tapper, *The Other Stratford*, West Ham Public Libraries Committee, 1962.

on behalf of all the clergy, Nonconformist ministers and Catholic priests as well as various local employers and school teachers.

The main objections raised by Pelly were that a theatre would have a detrimental effect on the moral elevation and become the resort of the lowest characters of the neighbourhood. Property prices would fall as a result, and concern was also expressed for the inhabitants of the nearby Home for Respectable Gentlewomen, who had, it was felt, little chance of remaining respectable if actors were unleashed near their home. (Sadly, we have no recorded comment from the said Respectable Gentlewomen!)

Pelly concluded by saying that the local West Ham Stipendiary Magistrate had informed him that there were many cases before the courts of children 'who had robbed their parents in order to go to miserable theatre'. But despite such strong opposition the Chairman of the Bench deemed that it was easier to keep control over a licensed permanent theatre than over a part-time movable fit-up, and granted, to Mr Charles Dillon, the licence for the new theatre.

Dillon had already decided on the site for his Playhouse, a wheelwright's shop in Salway Road owned by Mr James Foster. The architect chosen was James George Buckle who had recently designed the New Princess's Theatre in Oxford Street, central London (now demolished). Buckle's original plan was quite simple; he had proposed, on the basis of cost, to build the auditorium and stage inside the existing structure of the wheelwright's shop. The West Ham Local Board refused to pass this plan, however, on the grounds that it was altogether 'Unsafe' and 'Improper'. So Buckle had to return to his drawing board and re-design.

Buckle's original design for the Theatre Royal

During this process it was discovered upon inspection that the side wall on Salway Road was very solid and in good order, and so, mindful of costs, it was retained as the façade of the building in the amended plans, with the auditorium built onto it. With the licence granted and these amended plans passed the Theatre Royal was built in just over three months at a cost of little more than 3,000 pounds, by Messrs. David G. Laing & Sons of Duke Street, The Strand, London. You can see that original wall today, as it is still the front wall of the Theatre.

The Theatre's Grand Opening night was held on Wednesday, 17 December 1884 with a production of *Richelieu* or *The Conspiracy* by Lord Bulwer Lytton. Dillon chose the play because it was an established favourite with Victorian audiences and in the repertoire

DETAILS OF THE BUILDING OF THE THEATRE ROYAL, SALWAY ROAD, STRATFORD. E15

Designed by:	James George Buckle A.R.I.B.A.
Built by:	David G. Laing & Sons, Duke Street, Strand, London
Gas Arrangements:	Messrs Vaughan and Brown, Farringdon Road
Stage Machinery:	Mr. W. Wood, Strand Theatre, London.
Scenery by:	Messrs Freeman, Phillips and Assistants
Decorations & Upholstery:	Msr. Fardell, London and Paris
Carpeting, Curtains etc.	J. R. Roberts, Broadway, Stratford.
Furniture:	Mr. Butler
Lessee and Manager:	Mr. William Charles Dillon
Scenic Artist:	Mr. Cecil Hicks, Drury Lane.
Stage Carpenter:	Mr. William Thompson
Property Master:	Mr. A. Letts
Bill Inspector:	Mr. C. Perry
Musical Director:	Mr. Edward Bell
Gas and Limelight:	Mr. Fraser
Acting and Stage Manager:	Mr. Fred Thomas
Opened	Wednesday 17th December 1884

of most leading managements of the day. Dillon himself played the leading role of Cardinal Richelieu.

The local critics were favourably impressed, but the audience in the Gallery cracked nuts throughout the

OPENING PRODUCTION OF THE THEATRE ROYAL

'RICHELIEU' or 'THE CONSPIRACY'
by Lord Bulwer Lytton

Cast

Louis the Thirteenth	Mr. Archibald Graysdell
Gaston, Duke of Orléans	Mr. A. Munro
Baradas	Mr. G. W. Innes
Cardinal Richelieu	Mr. Charles Dillon
Chevalier de Mauprat	Mr. Frederick Thomas
Sieur de Beringhen	Mr. J. Keer
Joseph	Mr. Charles Horsman
Huguet	Mr. Arthur Cleveland
François	Miss Georgina Mansfield
Clermont	Miss Maude Woods
Captain of the Archers	Miss M. Harding
First, Second and Third)	Messrs Wallace, Leach
Secretaries of State)	and Vaughan
Julie de Mortemar	Miss Blanche Elliot
Marion de Lorme	Miss Nellie Horsman

Courtiers, Pages, Conspirators, Officers, Soldiers etc.

Followed by: A Comedietta............. Miss Lucy Hawthorns
Gertrude (with songs) Supported by the
Company

Dresses by.. W. C. Stinchcombe of
Drury Lane
Musical Conductor............................ Mr. A. F. Aldridge

Prices: Private Boxes: 21s. and 15s. a single seat: 2s.6d.
Circle: 2s. Stalls: 1s.6d. Pit: 1s. Gallery: 6d.

early scenes, so that Dillon had to appear before the curtain and rebuke them:

> You treat me fairly and I will treat you fairly and will give you good entertainment. But I will not have the beautiful lines of this play spoiled and my artistes insulted by your rude behaviour.

This speech was greeted by loud applause from the remainder of the house. The play was so successful it was brought back on numerous occasions.

The first reviews of the Grand Opening mention the fact that the outside of the building was rather dull— one review went so far as to dismiss the exterior as 'Ugly'—but there was universal praise from all quarters that spirits were lifted by the opulence of the interior.

> The auditorium is of the usual shape, and the tiers are so arranged that a good view of the stage is obtainable from every part. Above the Pit, on the first floor is a commodious Circle, the seats of which are plush-covered. The Gallery is situated above the Circle, and three handsomely fitted Boxes are arranged on either side and in close proximity to the stage. The general decorations are light, handsome and pleasing, of fleur-de-lis patterns and uniform design. The ceiling is also very prettily decorated. The Theatre is both handsome and comfortable.

As an event of considerable local importance the opening night was well covered by the *Stratford Express* in its issue of 20 December 1884. The main Editorial commented:

The so-called Theatre Royal, Stratford, has been opened this week. We are not aware of any solid ground for its adoption of the Royal title: and if it is a prophecy we are afraid it is a rather hardy one. If it is used to give an impression that the management desires to give only good plays and to make the Theatre really creditable to Stratford, we hail the promise with pleasure. And it is only fair to admit that the new theatre has on the whole commenced very well. A number of legitimate dramas shall be played. These are things, which do certainly show a determination to appeal to the best instincts of playgoers and to make the Theatre a home for the drama as distinguished from the dreary pieces in which the uninstructed delight to witness a murder every twenty minutes.

With the large population around it and the far greater population which can easily reach it by rail, the Stratford Theatre Royal appears to have a very good chance of becoming a financial success, and at the same time, conciliating the good opinion of many who now look upon the venture with coldness and doubt.

After his initial efforts, Dillon flung himself into his management with terrific energy and ran very successful seasons. However, although artistically very sound, he was no businessman. After eighteen months he found it an impossible task to balance the books, and sold out to Albert Fredericks, whose brother Frederick was married to Charles' sister Emily. Fredericks, a fairly prosperous coal merchant, had been helping his brother-in-law out financially from time to time, and the idea of taking over the Theatre appealed to him.

Fredericks immediately set about putting the Theatre on a proper commercial basis. The programming was handed over to Fred Thomas, a veteran actor who had both performed and stage-managed at the venue since its opening. The Theatre prospered as the quality of the shows improved, and received a better press than it had under Dillon. The *Stratford Express* commented that

> Great Pains have been taken by the management to meet the wishes of the public and they responded warmly, and good houses have been the rule.

The Theatre remained in the hands of the Fredericks family for nearly fifty years; their initials are to be seen either side of the cartouche above the Proscenium Arch.

In July 1887 Fred Thomas brought the forerunner of the moving pictures to the Royal—'Poole's Grand Dioramic Excursions'.[2] Huge pictures were shown on

---

2   The Diorama was invented by Louis Daguerre and Charles Bouton.

The front of house in 1990

translucent material with a painting on each side. By light manipulation on and through this flat surface the spectators could be convinced they were seeing life-size three-dimensional scenes changing with time. It was the painters' 3-D cinema. This spectacle attracted large audiences:

> Scenes placed on canvas are most realistic. The principal cities, places and towns throughout the world are visited and some clever mechanical effects are introduced.

Toward the end of 1887 Fredericks purchased two of the terraced houses adjoining the Theatre in Salway Road, demolished them and built onto the existing theatre structure a Workshop with Dressing Rooms above. Dressing Rooms were a luxury, for until this time the

61 Angel Lane. The arched windows show the office which is still used by the Theatre Royal's Artistic Director

performers had changed under the stage using 'orange boxes' as furniture.

After the huge success and packed houses that greeted the English Opera Company during the 1888–9 season, Fredericks decided the time was right to build a new and larger Theatre on Stratford Broadway, and he commissioned the great theatre designer Frank Matcham to design this new 'Broadway Theatre and Opera House'. Passing the day-to-day running of the Theatre Royal over to his brother Sam, he negotiated the purchase in 1891 of the Fish shop at 61 Angel Lane, rented until this time by Mr George Francis. The land belonging to this property lay at the rear of the stage, and after demolition it provided space and opportunity for various developments and extensions, traces of which are still visible today.

Firstly, it provided space for a long bar on the ground floor. The footprint of the original long bar can be seen today, as its mosaic tiled floor, which extended from the foyer into the Bar, is still intact. The space above the long bar was allocated to another bar for the Circle, more dressing rooms and an office overlooking Angel Lane for Fred Fredericks, which is still used by our current Artistic Director. Most importantly the purchase of the fish shop and its land meant that the depth of the stage could be extended from 18 feet to its present depth of 38 feet. The division between old and new stage can still be seen, and its back wall, like our front one, is intact. For the width of the Proscenium Arch we have one of the deepest stages in London!

To match the new stage a new front curtain was designed and painted by the Royal's resident scenic artist Arthur Hillyard, assisted by William Fredericks. The enlarged stage was used for the first time with a production of *The New Mazeppa* on 11 April 1891.

When Albert Fredericks died on 26 June 1901 control of the Theatre passed to his niece Caroline Fredericks Ellis. She was Frederick Fredericks' oldest child, and she was helped in the management of the Theatre by her brothers Frederick (junior) and Samuel. One of her first concerns was to modernise the Royal, and she applied to West Ham Borough Council for a supply of 'Electric Current' to be connected to the Theatre. She chose Frank Matcham (who had recently designed the Borough Theatre and Opera House for Albert on Stratford Broadway) to carry out these works of electrification and also 'to entirely re-upholster, re-seat and carpet the Theatre to make it one of the handsomest and cosiest of suburban theatres.'

The Theatre was closed for just a month for these installations and it reopened on the 12 May 1902. The reports of the reopening stated that

> The Theatre, by the alterations, has been considerably improved. A new Box Office is placed in the entrance, improvement has also been made to the vestibule, Panel mirrors have been introduced with fine effect. While in the building proper everything is most comfortable. In the Dress Circle the old seats have given place to excellent rows of Tip-up seats in Morocco Leather, provided and fixed by Robert's Stores Ltd. The whole of the Gallery has been rebuilt. Two new Boxes have been added, which are draped with dark red plush Curtains.
>
> The walls throughout the house covered with Incrusta linings, with dark Red groundwork and gilt flower patterns—the Dado rail down to the skirting being Fancy tiles carried all around the house giving a very pretty effect.
>
> The Pit has been dispensed with entirely, and now contains Stalls, known as 'Pit-Stalls' while a new drop-curtain has been added, the painting of which does credit to the local artist, Mr Arthur Hillyard, the theatre's permanent scenic artist.
>
> Carpets laid in every part of the house are stout Brussels supplied together with the draperies, upholstering and linoleums by the Hackney

Furnishing Company. Messrs Gibbs and Company have carried out the structural alterations and the decorations have been entrusted to Messrs De Jong. Electric light throughout gives the building the imposing appearance of a West End theatre.

The panel mirrors in the foyer

The 'Boxes' mentioned above have in recent times created rather a mystery. The review previously quoted of the Grand Opening of December 1884 (see page 18) suggests that 'three handsomely fitted boxes are arranged on either side and in close proximity to the stage'. In the review of the refurbishment of May 1902, however, we note that 'Two new Boxes were added ... which are draped with dark red plush Curtains'. These together with the original three mentioned in the report of the Opening in 1884 give the image of a very crowded auditorium, and we have no recorded evidence of boxes being 'removed'! Neither in this nor in the original report of 1884 is there any mention of 'where' the Boxes were situated, only that they were 'in close proximity of the stage'. Were the original Boxes on the Gallery level or vertically aligned?

Axel Burrough of Architects Levitt Bernstein Associates, who was in charge of both the refurbishment of the Auditorium in 1993 and the major rebuilding programme in 2001, considers it unlikely that 'in 1884 access to an expensive Box would be negotiated through the poorer classes in "The Pit"'. But perhaps Frank Matcham's up-market improvement of dispensing with the Pit and turning it into respectable 'Pit-Stalls' would have allowed his 'Two new Boxes draped with dark red plush Curtains' to be added to the stalls level? We shall return to the subject later.

In February and March 1907, in addition to the usual melodramas, 'Bioscope' pictures were included in the programme. In 1909 it was advertised that the Cup-tie Final played on 20 April between West Ham and Newcastle United would be reproduced the same night and nightly during the following week. Sadly for our local patrons the home side lost 2-1.

The Great War of 1914-18 seems to have made little difference to the Royal, except that the programming reflected the situation, for it remained open through-out the period of hostilities. The prices were raised, in common with all other places of entertainment, because of the levying by the Government of an Entertainment Tax, but otherwise it seemed to be business as usual.

More calamitous for the Theatre, perhaps, were the events of Bank Holiday Monday, August 1921, when fire broke out at the Royal. Caroline's brother Fred was licensee at the time. The Fire Officer's report states:

2nd August at 12.01am—a serious fire occurred at the Theatre Royal, Salway Road, Stratford. The stage scenery, dock and back portions of the premises and contents were very severely damaged by fire. Smoke and water damaged the rest of the premises including the auditorium, dressing rooms and contents.

The report in the *Stratford Express* was somewhat more graphic:

Considerable excitement prevailed in the neighbourhood of the Theatre Royal on Monday night when it was discovered that the building was on fire. There had been the usual performance during the evening and when the audience left everything was as usual. At about midnight however smoke was seen issuing from the stage end of the Theatre and the West Ham Fire Brigade was immediately called both by a stranger and by the night staff of the telephone exchange opposite, who had seen the glare of the flames. A general call to the West Ham Fire Brigade station was given and three motor pumps and two escapes were quickly in attendance.

On their arrival the firemen found the stage and scenery were involved and the stage area enveloped by dense clouds of smoke. The value of the safety curtain was demonstrated by the fact that it had prevented the fire from spreading to the auditorium. The firemen experienced considerable difficulty in combating the fire because of the dense smoke, but they concentrated their efforts upon the flames spreading to the hall and in this they were entirely successful. It was only after an hour's hard work that they were able to get the fire under control, and altogether it was three and half-hours before they were able to leave the scene.

The Royal reopened on 16 January 1922 with its usual programming. However, the East End at this time was now going through a difficult post-war depression. A large proportion of the male population was out of work and on some form of relief. Visits to the Theatre were becoming more of a luxury, especially as the Theatre was now competing with Public Sound Broadcasting and finding it very difficult matching the 'gloss' of the cinema with its star names and realistic productions.

The Royal closed its doors in the same week that the General Strike hit Britain in May of 1926.

Various attempts were made to attract an audience but all ended with repeated closure. In the summer of 1932 Fred Fredericks Jr decided to try a different sort of programme. Drama had failed but he was determined to offer Stratford an alternative to the cinema, which by now was offering the 'Talkies'. He reopened the doors on 5 September with a series of revues and variety performances. Sadly the programme did not attract the Stratford audience and after only five weeks the Royal was once again dark.

This period marked the end of an era. Frederick Fredericks Jr, now 68 years old, decided to retire. The

Royal had been under the active management of the Fredericks family for nearly fifty years and they had carried on the traditions with which they had grown up in the heyday of the stock company. But the mood of the public had changed, and there were no sons who might change the policy of the Theatre to match that mood. Fred Jr was to be the last member of that famous and respected East End theatrical family to manage the Royal.

The lease of the Theatre passed to Sam Frederick's daughters Mrs Ivy Webster and Mrs Gwendoline Thompson. Many brave attempts were made to revitalise the Theatre but none were successful for any length of time. In September 1939, with the advent of the Second World War, all theatres closed for a short period as part of government policy to keep crowds from gathering in case of large-scale air raids on London. Any further ideas that there might have been about reopening the Royal had to be shelved.

The Theatre remained closed until March 1943, when it was re-licensed to J. Rowland Sales Ltd on behalf of Music Halls Consolidated. The Theatre by this time was in a dreadful condition. Parts of the stage floor were broken, most of the windows had been smashed, seats had been ripped and the paintwork was peeling. George James Buckle's original structure had stood the test of sixty years, but a considerable amount of money had to be spent to put the Theatre back into working order.

On 29 March 1943 the Mayor of West Ham (Alderman A.W. Wells, JP) performed the opening ceremony, as the Royal reopened its doors as a 'Variety and Revue

Theatre'. It was wartime and it was hoped that people would prefer some form of escapist entertainment. And so the Royal provided a series of revues. 'Nice enough to be Naughty', 'Eve without Leaves', and 'Peaches and Pyjamas' among them. Sadly the venture did not appeal to the local audience, and the Theatre once more closed its doors on 3 June 1944. J. Rowland Sales Ltd contemplated turning the Theatre into a 'first-class dance hall' (similar perhaps to Drury Lane's 'Lyceum' which had become a Mecca Dance Hall), but the idea fell through, possibly because the Theatre's position at that time was considered unsuitable.

The next Knight on a White Charger to take up the challenge of managing the Royal was the author Evelyn Dysart. He returned the Royal to its position as a 'Playhouse', telling the *Stratford Express* 'I aim to make this theatre the repertory home for the District. We do not intend to depart from a high standard and each week will stage a West End play. From time to time we shall augment our company with well-known guest players'. Well intentioned though his sentiments may have been they were to little avail. It was a nerve-wracking time for the populace of the East End. The German Flying Bombs and later V-2 Rockets that dropped from the sky and exploded with no warning gave very little incentive for people to venture out for an evening's entertainment. So once again the Theatre closed its doors but this time for a longer period, from March of 1945 until November 1946.

On 1 October 1946 David Horne applied for and was granted the licence of the Theatre. He had acquired the lease then held by Mrs Marion Fredericks Tagg and hoped to establish his own repertory company. He was the first actor-manager to take over the Theatre since the Fredericks.

He found the building again in very bad condition: little maintenance had been carried out in the preceding years. The roof and the back wall of the stage were weak as a result of bombing in the area and had to be strengthened. Most of the seats in the auditorium needed renewing and the electric wiring looked as though it had not been touched since it was first installed 44 years previously. Indeed, it very probably had not!

He sectioned off part of the Stalls long bar with a partition for the sale of soft drinks and sandwiches. This space, known as the 'Coffee Bar', was still in place until the refurbishment in 1993, and indeed was the forerunner of today's food counter. His other major installation was a Scene Dock and Paint Frame in a bay on stage right. The bay had been used for the stabling of animals used in various variety acts and for a Circus that had appeared at the Royal, and was in a filthy and smelly condition. Some years ago a member of our audience told me that as a small boy his father had brought him to the Royal to see the Circus. The only clear memory he had of the evening was that of the 'Performing Monkey'. 'I can still see it,' he told me, 'and the thought of it still makes me laugh,' as indeed he did. Sadly, my enquiries have not been able to locate a copy of the programme for our archive.

The Theatre reopened as a Playhouse on Monday, 4 November 1946, with Arthur Pinero's *The Second Mrs Tanqueray*. David Horne maintained a high standard of plays and ran very successful seasons at the Royal. However, this was the time when cinema was fighting hard against re-established television services. Cinema experimented with 3-D, wide screens and improved colour and theatres all over the country once again found it hard to compete. Horne had used a great deal of his own money in supporting his seasons, but after three years could no longer afford the finance and decided the time had come to stop.

Horne was very philosophical about the venture. 'We tried hard,' he said, 'and never relaxed from the standard that we had set ourselves. It was a combination of circumstances which defeated us, and we were very sorry that we had to leave the Royal. It is a nice little theatre, built by an actor for himself. We look back with affection to the time that we spent there.'

Gabriel Toyne and his wife Diana Beaumont leased the Theatre from Horne for its last four week period. Both had worked with Horne during his occupancy of the Royal, Toyne as a producer and Beaumont as actress in his last three plays. History was to record a very significant four weeks!

Toyne and Beaumont presented Anthony Kimmins' *While Parents Sleep*, Beaumont in the role she had created in the original production and Toyne as her husband. A new management, a new play: the locals did not rush to support it.

The company played for two weeks before deciding that they could not run for a third. During their meeting to discuss what shows they could get in at short notice a call came through from a Gerald Raffles, General Manager for The Theatre Workshop Company. That company was touring a Christmas production of *Alice in Wonderland*. Had Toyne a free week at the Royal? The deal was clinched over the telephone, and thus the company who a few years later were to return and make the Theatre Royal Stratford-atte-Bow world famous appeared there for the first time.

For the last week of their management, the Toynes presented Tod Slaughter in *Spring-Heeled Jack, the Terror of Epping Forest*. The opening performance of Monday 16 January 1950 was transmitted live, presented by Peter Dimmock, for the BBC, the first live television transmission from the Theatre Royal. So in their four week management period the Toynes had introduced Theatre Workshop to Stratford and also pioneered live broadcasts!

In the next three years three separate managements endeavoured to bring the Royal back to life, including Rowland Sales who once again took up the gauntlet. They reopened as a 'Palace of Varieties' but the family audiences of previous years were lost: families were watching television and the teenagers were rock'n'rollin' and so the audience again failed to materialise. Sales' final show was Paul Raymond's Review 'Jane comes to Town' which closed on 24 January 1953.

A week later an experimental theatre company opened for a six-week season of plays. This was the returning Theatre Workshop Company, directed by Joan Littlewood with Gerald C. Raffles, a member of the Company, as General Manager. It was six weeks that

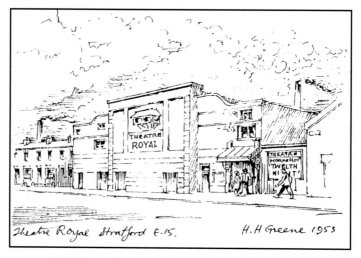

The Theatre Royal drawn by Harry H. Greene in 1953

have never ended. The Theatre Workshop Company was to stay and eventually buy the lease of the Theatre from Mrs Ivy Webster.

The decision to rent and then lease the Theatre Royal was a major one for the Company. It was the first time they had had a theatre as a permanent base, having been a touring ensemble until that time. Apart from their time spent at the Theatre Royal some three years earlier with *Alice in Wonderland*, they toured mostly in the North of England, Wales, Scotland and Europe. The Theatre Royal was once again in need of extensive repair, maintenance and decoration. No funds were available for all this work, so in between rehearsing the plays for the upcoming six week season, the company set to work themselves, cleaning and painting and trying to get the old boiler beneath the stage to work, which they generally failed to do. Meanwhile, although technically against the rules of their lease, they lived in the dressing rooms of the Theatre to save money they never had.

The Company opened on 2nd February 1953 with *Twelfth Night*, 'to a small but very enthusiastic audience'. It continued to rent the Theatre after its initial six weeks, implementing its originating policy in presenting the best of European and contemporary drama. Financial support was a dire necessity. The Company had survived on box office takings, which in those early days were very meagre, and lived as a commune, sharing the tasks of running the Theatre, and running a duty roster for Chef of the Week!

In April 1953 Gerry Raffles wrote to the local Town Clerk, suggesting that

> The Royal could become the Borough's Civic Theatre worthy of its place as the only theatre in the Borough

The reply stated that

> The Finance Committee at their last meeting was unable to recommend any grant for the purposes you have in mind. However, the Committee indicated that they would be prepared to assist where possible in the matter of publicity, providing this could be done without cost to the Committee.

Recognition came not from the local Boroughs, nor indeed from England or its Arts Council, but instead from the International Festival of Theatre in Paris. In 1955 the Festival's director, A.M. Julien, and his assistant

Claude Planson, who knew and admired the Company's work, invited them to the Paris World Theatre Season to represent England. The Company scraped together the money for a one way fare. Each member, with costumes in their suitcases, carried a piece of scenery or stage prop as hand luggage, much to the dismay of the airline staff, as many pieces of this 'hand luggage' were not only rather large but also very unusual!

The Theatre Workshop presented *Volpone* and *Arden of Faversham* in May 1955 at the Théâtre Hébertot, taking Paris by storm. The French critics raved. One wrote, 'We do not possess a single company in France comparable to this one. Nothing which resembles its ardour, its generosity, and, to say all, its youth. You have set the Festival of Paris alight in its first week. We salute you with joy as being the purist, the simplest, and the greatest artists'. Money was raised in Paris for their return fare, and the Company arrived back at the Theatre Royal covered in glory, though still penniless.

England, its Arts Council and the local Boroughs began to be aware that they had an internationally-famed company resident at the Theatre Royal, Stratford-atte-Bow. So, gradually, did the theatre critics. Financial aid began to arrive from the surrounding local Borough Councils, and these, though small, were very welcome, as were the increasing audiences taking an interest in this rare Company.

The Company's lease of the Theatre expired on 10 June 1956. Charles Webster, the husband of Fred Fredericks' daughter Ivy and trustee of the Caroline Ellis-

Fredericks Trust, after protracted negotiations, allowed the Workshop to acquire the head-lease.

In 1958 two plays were presented that would transform the fortunes of the Theatre Royal and the Theatre Workshop Company, Shelagh Delaney's *A Taste of Honey* and Brendan Behan's *The Hostage*. These two productions both transferred the following year to the Wyndhams Theatre, Charing Cross Road, allowing Gerry Raffles to spend some money on the fabric of the Royal.

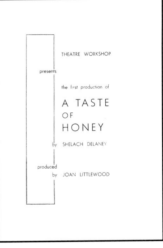

He put into action plans for a new Green Room, the actors' relaxation and meetings area. This was a major project. The old one until this time had been a dark internal room some twelve feet square, with a low ceiling, a naked electric light bulb and a piece of ancient rush matting on the floor. In one corner was a small table on which sat a gas ring. Tea, sometimes for a cast of up to sixteen people, as well as the hot water for washing up, all came from that single gas ring. It was also a source of heating for frozen actors during rehearsals in the winter (the old boiler underneath the stage was only lit one hour before curtain up). Above this space, accessed by a verti-

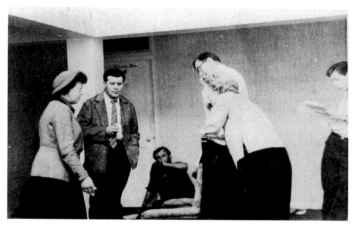

Above: Pre-Rehearsal in the new green room to work on script of Sparrers Can't Sing, *August 1960. Left to right: Joan Littlewood, Manfred Borge (visiting from Maxim Gorky, Berlin), John Wallbank (stage manager), Stephen Lewis (author), Bettina Dickson, Murray Melvin.*
Below: Four hours later. Left to right: Joan Littlewood, Manfred Borge, Murray Melvin , Stephen Lewis, Bettina Dickson.

cal ladder, was the Theatre's Prop Room, a window from which led out to the roof area. A corridor ran on two sides of the old Green Room, one connecting the main staircase to the foyer, the other leading to the dressing rooms and offices that had been built by Albert Fredericks on the site of the Angel Lane Fish shop in 1891.

All this was swept away. The whole space was opened up to double height with windows lighting the whole area. A proper kitchen with constant hot water was also added. It was a transformation scene worthy of our Pantomime! Finally green carpet was laid over the whole area, which I am certain matched the 'stout Brussels' mentioned in the Matcham refurbishment of 1902 (see page 24).

In 1959 came the transfer of the next successful production *Make me an Offer*, soon to be followed in 1960 by the Lionel Bart musical *Fings Ain't Wot They Used T'be*.

The Theatre building having grown piecemeal over the years, complex negotiations were necessary to obtain the freeholds of the various plots of land on which the Theatre stood. However, in 1961 Gerry Raffles started the first tentative moves to purchase these individual plots. It was to be a long and arduous task.

The original 1884 entrance canopy, seen in 1959.

Raffles also ordered at this time a new and modern canopy for the main entrance. It helped to keep people dry as they queued for returns, which was by then a nightly occurrence. A photograph of the original 1884 entrance canopy can be seen on the right-hand entrance wall to the Bar from the main foyer. On the left-hand wall is a photograph of Raffles' new one.

In the corridor to the toilets from the main bar is a photograph of the front of house, showing Raffles' new canopy as it was decorated for the legendary produc-

tion in 1963 of *Oh, What a Lovely War*. It is also interesting because it shows the houses adjoining the Theatre in Salway Road, two of which Albert Fredericks had purchased in 1887, also shown in the sketch by Harry Greene (see page 34).

During the run of *Oh, What a Lovely War*, as Gerry Raffles was showing Donald Albery the improvements he had started and those he wanted to make in the auditorium, he pointed to the ceiling at a very meagre light fitting suspended from the centre. 'I want to get a proper chandelier for there,' he said. Donald Albery was the Donmar Management, and had been responsible for taking *A Taste of Honey* and *The Hostage* into the Wyndhams Theatre at Charing Cross Road, which had been owned by his father, Sir Bronson Albery. 'Oh,' said Donald in response, 'you must have the other one of ours!' Explaining, he told Raffles 'When my Father bought the one we have hanging in Wyndhams, there

was a pair. The other one is still in boxes in the basement of the Theatre. I shall have it sent to you.' So the magnificent chandelier you see today hanging from the ceiling in the auditorium (a particularly fine view is to be had from the Upper Circle) has a double which is still in place at the Wyndhams theatre.

In 1967 after the successful transfer of *Mrs Wilson's Diary* to the West End and after six years of protracted negotiations Gerry Raffles had the wherewithal to complete the purchase of the Freehold for the last remaining plots on which the Theatre stood. With the success of the secured ownership of the Theatre came the announcement of the regeneration of the centre of Stratford, the plans for which would include the demolition of the area of Angel Lane and Salway Road, including the Theatre Royal. It was a bitter blow!

Gerry Raffles

Even as the bulldozers made their way along Angel Lane from Stratford Broadway, Gerry Raffles, who had already been doing everything in his power to hold up their advance, managed to obtain a provisional Grade II Preservation Order on the Theatre. The Department of the Environment's definition of Grade II listing states that

> These are buildings of special interest which warrant every effort being made to preserve them.

Nevertheless, there were persistent attempts by developers to have the Royal demolished. Raffles himself was on constant guard, nightly moving back the barriers placed against the walls of the Theatre by builders at the end of their working day, making sure that a bulldozer never 'accidentally' knocked down one of the supporting walls. Much to his credit his determined efforts saved his beloved Royal from the town planners.

Joan Littlewood defiant on the rocks

Meanwhile Joan Littlewood, with the help of young volunteers, cleared the rubble next to the Theatre that had been left by the demolition of Salway Road and started an Adventure Playground. The Theatre Workshop had always been involved in local activities for young people. Classes arranged in local schools involved imaginative game play. This was an early start to what is now known as 'Theatre in Education'. A group was started in the Theatre, eventually called 'The Nutters', who were allowed to perform their own shows on a Friday night between 6 and 8 o'clock. Later these shows were expanded and performed on Sundays.

Other regular groups of differing ages were formed, and some of the older participants encouraged to train in the various disciplines of the theatre. This policy still continues at the Theatre, where many of today's actors, directors, writers, technicians and administrators started in the Theatre Royal's youth groups.

Joan Littlewood devising games with boxes (above)
and with 'The Nutters' (below)

The Theatre Royal dwarfed by new office block, October 1975

After many years of effort Gerry Raffles at last obtained sufficient support from the funding bodies to start a full season of plays. These were to have a nucleus of the old company members, with everyone on proper salaries. This would stem the need to transfer plays to the West End in order that both the Theatre and the individual Company members could survive financially. The objective was to keep a fully trained Workshop Company at the Royal.

Preparations were under way for this exciting new season when tragically, at this highpoint for the Workshop Company and in the Theatre Royal's history, came the sudden and tragic death of Gerry Raffles on 11 April 1975 aged just 51. Joan Littlewood, grief stricken at the loss of her partner and her support, left the Theatre, never to return. The Square at the side of the Theatre was named in Gerry's honour and memory.

How ironic that, some 40 years later as part of yet another rebuilding programme, a more enlightened local authority saw the potential that Gerry had envisaged and designated the area as 'Stratford's Cultural Quarter'!

Gerry's photograph and dedication are to be found in the entrance to the Bar from Gerry Raffles Square. The street sign, under his photograph, was retrieved from the original square that was demolished in the rebuilding programme of 2001. He is also among the many photographs of Workshop productions that decorate the Bar.

Following the sudden departure of Joan Littlewood various people took over the direction of the Theatre for short periods. Ken Hill, who had been working as writer, director and actor for the company was followed by Maxwell Shaw, a long-standing member of the Theatre Workshop. He in turn was followed by Clare Venables, and then in 1979 by Philip Hedley, who kept the Theatre open and vibrant for the next 25 years.

In June 1992, with new high-rise office buildings dominating the Royal, a new canopy designed by the Theatre's Associate Designer Jenny Tiramani was unveiled, which gave the entrance to the Theatre a new significance. A photograph of this latest canopy can be seen on the left-hand wall of the entrance to the Bar from the foyer.

Canopy designed by Jenny Tiramani, 1992

Plans were also made at this time to move the Bar. The opposite wall of the Bar on the front of the building had a narrow strip of land available. This space was incorporated into the building, and the Bar transferred there from its original position and then lengthened. There is a photograph of the original Bar taken in the 1950's on the left-hand pillar of the present-day Bar counter. It shows Ruth and Bill Parham who were in charge of the Bar in those days. You will also see the partition behind which was the Coffee Bar area installed by David Horne in 1946.

A photograph of the new 1990's Bar can be seen on the right-hand wall at the entrance from the Foyer. You will also notice on the left-hand side of the photograph that the original Bar wall fixture had been left in situ.

In 1993 a major grant was obtained for the refurbishment of the auditorium. This was funded by the Stratford City Challenge Initiative, the Department of National Heritage, and the Theatre's own fundraising activities. The work was undertaken by Levitt Bernstein Associates Ltd.

A major addition at the centre back of the Gallery was a Lighting and Sound Box. The Gallery was stripped of its bare wooden benches and replaced by upholstered seating. During this work, in between the joists of the flooring were found heaps of broken walnut shells. Some of these I have placed in the archive of the Theatre in the hope that they may have been those very nuts being cracked during the opening performance of *Richelieu* in 1884 that had caused Charles Dillon to stop the show to admonish the audience (see page 18).

The walls around the Stalls and Circle had over the years been covered in many layers of wallpaper, each layer having been painted over with what was then called 'Distemper', the forerunner of today's emulsion paint. The last layer had been a deep plum colour, very rich if somewhat sober. Gerry Raffles had purchased this paint at cut price when the local 'Oil Shop' in Angel Lane (a photograph of which can be seen at the end of the food counter) had an end of range sale and. The shopkeeper I believe had been mighty relieved to be rid of it! As a background to our much-worn deep red plush seating I think it looked rather grand, if redolent of a somewhat faded grandeur, but by the late 90s it had had its day.

It was the intention to remove these many layers of wallpaper to be replaced by a thick embossed covering called Anaglypta. However, when the builders stripped down the old paper (all eleven layers!) they discovered the original wooden wall coverings. These were simply painted pine tongue and grooving, but as decoration these had at the base of each section, next to the dado rail, a stenciled pattern, then still visible though with very faint colouring. It was the same in the Circle, though the pattern there was not so elaborate as that in the Stalls, which became known as our 'Elongated Pineapple'.

Plans were changed, the Anaglypta cancelled, the tongue and grooving repaired where necessary and our Theatre painted red. Stencils were made of both the original patterns in the Stalls and Circle and transferred to the newly painted wood, and the result can be seen in today's Auditorium. Similar restoration has taken place on the mainstaircase.

In the Stalls all the seating had been removed to be repaired and recovered. Certain floorboards were to be removed to allow trunking for extra electrical cables to be installed between joists. Upon inspection, Levitt Bernstein Associates considered these solid oak floor-boards to be in excellent condition after 109 years' service. A special grant was obtained for extra labour costs, in order that due time and care could be taken not only in raising the historic boards but returning them without damage. It was Levitt Berstein's opinion that they would be good for another 100 years or more.

*Pieces of the broken tiles discovered in the rear Stalls, and the frieze design
derived from them and painted around the walls of the Stalls area.*

It was during this work that we discovered in the rear Stalls, yet again between joists, a heap of broken tiles, the Tiler's cast-offs neatly swept into a pile at the end of their working day. Tiles! One's memory leapt to that review of the Matcham refurbishment of 1902: '...the Dado rail down to the skirting being Fancy Tiles' (see page 24). This was the first sight of these tiles there had been in recent history. Luckily there was an almost undamaged tile among the many pieces, which is now in the Theatre's Archive. To commemorate this important find, a frieze was printed of the tile pattern and an extra smaller rail added below the dado around the walls of the Stalls area. This frieze can be seen between these rails.

The remaining pieces of tile were sealed in a very strong plastic envelope together with a letter telling of our joy and excitement at the discovery of this 'hoard' and explaining the commemorative frieze around the walls. This package was replaced between the exact joists where they were found, followed by the relaying of the very large and heavy oak flooring, and it is our hope that in another hundred years the same discovery will give as much pleasure as it gave us in 1993.

Once again during this refurbishment the conundrum of the Boxes arose. If you look at both the Circle and Gallery horseshoes sloping to the Proscenium arch you will see the 'join' between the original decoration and the Boxes. It is a rather brutal join and certainly the decoration does not match. I can hardly believe James George Buckle responsible for such an odd design flaw in his original plans. The review of the Matcham refurbishment of 1902 (see page 24) states that 'the whole of

53

the Gallery has been rebuilt'. Was this alteration necessitated by the new Cupola structure over the Gallery
Box, and then carried down to the Circle, and together

*The 'strange empty area' under the Circle boxes prior to the installation of
the Stalls boxes in 1993.*

with the improvements made in the new rather grand Pit-Stalls, into the Stalls area?

We have no record or reports of Boxes being 'removed' from the Stalls area before or after the Matcham improvements so for the present this remains a mystery, but during this most recent refurbishment, guided by Axel Burrough of Levitt Bernstein Associates, a Stalls Box on each side of the Auditorium was designed, built and fitted. Immediately they were in place the whole auditorium took on a perfect balance; it then seemed obvious that they should be there, and indeed may have been there before in a different form.

When I first started at the Royal as a student in 1957 and up to the 1993 refurbishment the seating in the Stalls was in straight lines directly across the auditorium (see the seating plan in the old box office). There was a strange empty area either side of the Stalls, under the Circle boxes, next to the Proscenium Arch, which always struck me as rather odd (see the photograph on the opposite page). I think it significant that during our 1993 refurbishment when the Stall Boxes were installed the seating had to be changed to a gentle curve, to accommodate the boxes and also the sight lines for the audience to the stage. This repositioning meant the loss of some fourteen seats. It is my belief that in the Royal's heyday of attendance, sometime after the Matcham alterations, the Stalls Boxes were removed without ceremony in order to increase revenue and more seats added in their place, economics ruling the day rather than any aesthetic consideration.

I can find no recorded proof for this theory, which is just my conjecture. However, whatever the truth behind this puzzle the Axel Burrough addition makes the interior look perfect.

On 16 December 1993 after the completion of this refurbishment the original Preservation Order obtained by Gerry Raffles in 1972 was upgraded to Grade II*. The definition of 'Grade Two, Starred' reads:

> These are particularly important buildings of more than special interest.

Gerry Raffles would have been justly proud.

In 1999 a London Borough of Newham Capital project, with the Arts Council of England Lottery Department and Stratford City Challenge, led to the next regeneration of the Salway Road and Gerry Raffles Square area. This was then renamed 'Stratford's Cultural Quarter' and included a new Cinema and Performing Arts Centre (now known as Stratford Circus) adjacent and attached to the Theatre in Salway Road, to be run by the Local Authority. For the Theatre it meant a great deal of additional building, providing much-needed extra space for offices and dressing rooms to accommodate our ever-expanding training and educational programmes. Of course, none of this alteration affected the listed structure.

Levitt Bernstein Associates were again in charge of the project, which would incorporate the combined building of the Performing Arts Centre in Salway Road and the alterations and additions to the Royal. The Builders undertaking the work were YJL Construction Ltd. The plan was to close the Theatre after the pantomime *Hansel and Gretel* in February 1998 and to reopen with the new pantomime the following December. Offices were rented above a local builders' merchant in Grove Crescent Road a short distance from the Theatre. The entire contents of the Theatre were put into store, a massive task for all the staff. The Royal's community and educational work was continued, touring schools and local community centres, during this enforced absence.

The summer came and no work had started on the Theatre! Our local community was in danger of losing their annual pantomime. The Artistic Director and the Board of Directors took the decision, against advice from the authorities, to reopen the Theatre and mount a pantomime for the Christmas 1998-99 season. *Cinderella* was chosen and opened on 1 December 1998. There was trepidation that after such a long closure our local audience might have made other arrangements for family entertainment over the Christmas season, but great relief all round when the attendance figures were record breaking!

Once more, on 29 February 1999 the Theatre was given back to the builders and the various community outreach programmes continued to be organised from the temporary offices. The building and alterations work at last commenced, but delay followed delay with agonising regularity.

An extended and refurbished Theatre Royal eventually reopened its doors as originally intended with a Pantomime. *Aladdin* opened on 1 December 2001 with a full house—a new audience for the new Royal! The original ten month closure period had been stretched to nearly three years, one of the longest periods of closure in the Theatre Royal's history. But facilities in the Theatre had been greatly improved, with new rehearsal and office space, plus dressing rooms with the addition of heating and showers, luxuries that would have amazed the old players of the Royal.

The major rebuilding had provided two extra rehearsal rooms. The main room is dedicated to Philip Hedley who was the Artistic Director of the Theatre for twenty-five years from 1979 to 2004. The smaller room on the ground floor we have devoted to Charles Dillon; we have his photograph on the wall and underneath a dedication to him, and the room is now known affectionately as 'Dillon's'. Charlie may have left the scene early but without his inspiration and perseverance the building would not be here today.

Land at the rear of the building enabled a further extension to be built onto the back wall of our stage, which provides a corridor on both floors. Before this, the only way to get from one side of the stage to the other during a performance was by way of a treacherous low ceiling passage under the stage, or by going to front of house and across the Gallery.

Two very modern 'wings' have also been added to the sides of the building. Viewed from Theatre Square the left-hand wing has extended the area of the original houses that Albert Fredericks had purchased in 1887, giving us, like him, extra space for a modern workshop and paint room at the rear of the building. Also a backstage lift to all floors was installed for the use of our technical staff. 'Dillon's' Rehearsal room, with Production offices above, are at the front of this wing, and a new Fly Tower can be seen which allows for the eventual jump from 19th century flying mechanisms (with hemp ropes) to 21st century technology (computer controlled, powered winches). The roof area also houses new air-handling units for the building.

The right-hand wing provides a new enlarged Box Office at the entrance to the Theatre and above it a Circle Bar. This Bar has been dedicated to the memory of Ken Hill and the wonderful shows he has written and directed for the Theatre. The Bar is decorated with programmes and memorabilia of his productions.

The Foyer area has been increased: on the right-hand side the wall has been opened up to create a new space. The original Matcham 1902 panelled mirror has been transferred to the back wall of this area together with an original radiator made redundant from the Circle. It also houses a new lift to allow disabled access to all floors. This additional space is dedicated to the memory of Avis Bunnage, a long serving and much loved member of the Theatre Workshop Company, and is now known as 'Avis' Foyer'. On display is the dress she wore in the 'I'll Make a Man of You' sequence from the 1963 musical *Oh What a Lovely War*, plus the original designs by Una Collins of the costumes from that show. There is also a photograph of Avis as Marie Lloyd, and next to the lift one of her getting ready for a performance in her long-occupied old Dressing Room 4.

The two staircases from the Foyer to the circle feature posters and photographs from the Philip Hedley era.

The Stalls Bar has recently seen major alterations. With land available at the rear of the building the decision was taken to move the Bar yet again, this time back to its original position but again lengthened. Behind the Bar we now have a kitchen to allow cooked food to be made available all day to our patrons, a modern successor to David Horne's 1946 Coffee Bar and Sandwich area. The original glass-backed bar fixture has been saved and refitted onto the end wall, and can be seen as you enter the Bar from the Foyer. The extension has created a terrace opening onto Gerry Raffles Square, and also a small performance area for Bar entertainment. The Bar is dedicated to and called the 'Theatre Workshop Bar', and is decorated with photographs and memorabilia from its illustrious past.

Joan Littlewood died on 20 September 2002. With her passing the Theatre Royal's ownership was transferred, as was her wish, to the 'Theatre Workshop Trust', ensuring that the building would be in safe hands for the future.

In 2004 Philip Hedley's 25 year stewardship as Artistic Director came to an end. His Deputy Kerry Michael was appointed to the post.

And so after her many trials and tribulations and the momentous changes that have occurred in recent times the 'Royal' starts her 125th Anniversary burnished and replenished with a new young administration, who I know have due regard for the history of the building.

I am certain that Charles Dillon, the Fredericks family, G. Rowland Sales, Evelyn Dysart and David Horne would look on with pride and amazement. Not least Gerald C. Raffles, who at the very moment of the Theatre Royal's demise, saved her for the generations yet to come.

It is my fervent hope that if George James Buckle's structure gets through to its second centenary they will at the very least have fireworks!

Murray Melvin
Theatre Royal, Stratford, 2009

MURRAY MELVIN

Murray Melvin, with a small grant from the Co-operative Society to study drama for one year, became a student with the Theatre Workshop Company. Like all members of the Company, whether new or long standing, he discovered that the curriculum was not that of a normal stage training establishment. The intricate art of making sixteen cups of tea on one gas ring was quickly mastered. Then as a dogsbody to John Bury, the Company's Designer, he progressed to painting the red and gold Foyer and then the blue exterior of the building's façade. Mixing sand and cement and learning to pebble-dash theatre sets and erect scaffolding quickly followed the unblocking of drains.

Between all these activities, Murray was included in the Company's pre-rehearsal training sessions which included his introduction to the Laban technique of movement and voice. His first appearance on stage was as the Queen's Messenger in the then production-in-rehearsal of *Macbeth*. This was followed by small parts in other plays of the season, which included *You Won't Always be on Top*, a play about a building site – the whole Company having to go to a real one and learn bricklaying.

After the Christmas production playing Scrooge's Nephew in Dickens' *A Christmas Carol*, Murray then created the role of Jeffrey in Shelagh Delaney's *A Taste of Honey* which the following year transferred to the Wyndhams Theatre. He was to repeat this role in the film directed by Tony Richardson, for which he was awarded the Prix de Cannes at the Festival as Best

Actor. After *Honey* came the role of the soldier Leslie in Brendan Behan's *The Hostage*. William Saroyan came to London with his play *Sam, the Highest Jumper of them All*, and cast Murray as Sam. Murray first went to the Paris Festival with the Company as Brainworm in Ben Jonson's *Every Man in his Humour*. Back at Stratford he played the part of Knocker in Stephen Lewis's *Sparrers Can't Sing*, a role he reprised in the film version directed by Joan Littlewood.

The last time he appeared with the Company was in the First World War Musical *Oh, What a Lovely War*, which played in London, the Paris Festival and New York. His films include *Alfie, The Devils, Barry Lyndon, Ghost Story, Start the Revolution Without Me, The Boyfriend, Comrades* and *The Phantom of the Opera*.

Murray was a founder member of The Actors Centre and was its Chairman for four years, during which time he initiated a Branch of the Centre in Manchester in honour of Joan and the Workshop.

In 1990 Murray started to collate an archive of the Theatre Workshop residency at the Theatre Royal. This work has now extended to include the whole period of the Theatre's existence.

Murray was invited to become a member of the Board of the Theatre Royal in 1991; he is also a guardian of the Theatre Workshop Trust.